Table of Contents

Chapter 1: Aquarius Personality Profile

Ruling Planet: Uranus

Symbol: the water bearer

Element: air

Quality: fixed

Traits: eccentric, emotionally detached, extroverted, generous, humanitarian, idealistic, imprudent, independent, innovative, intellectual, open-minded, optimistic, original, progressive, rebellious, restless, sensation-seeking, stubborn, tactless, unpredictable

Eccentric

Aquarians are the quirky eccentrics of the zodiac. They gravitate to brilliant, unconventional companions, and if they find their friends or lovers too ordinary and predictable, they'll usually wander off in search of more stimulating company. However, when they find people who meet their odd standards, they tend to be very loyal.

Aquarians also gravitate to unusual interests and pastimes, acquiring eclectic collections of objects associated with various hobbies and obsessions, as they are always trying new things. These collections usually end up piled in closets or strewn haphazardly around the home unless the Aquarius has a rising sign more inclined toward tidiness, such as Libra, Virgo, Scorpio, or Capricorn (see Appendix 2 for information on how to find your rising sign, moon sign, and other planetary placements in your natal zodiac).

Aquarians personify the absentminded professor, frequently lost in worlds of their own, often contemplating brilliant ideas. Their original minds make them interesting and thought-provoking companions.

Emotionally detached

Aquarians process feelings intellectually rather than emotionally. They like to think things through, come up with rational, logical solutions, and talk about issues in a calm, detached way. This emotional style can be distressing for more sensitive types, leading to clashes if the Aquarian tries to address an issue with logic when others just want to express their feelings.

Because Aquarians tend to be so calm and unemotional, more volatile companions may verbally harass them in the hope of provoking an emotional response, but an Aquarian is more likely to retreat in irritation than be drawn into battle. Aquarians enjoy debating issues as an intellectual exercise, but they dislike fighting with people who become irrational and emotionally expressive. It is far easier to win an Aquarian over to your point of view by making a well-reasoned argument than with crying or raging.

Many Aquarians are so out of touch with their feelings that they don't notice they are distressed about something until they experience physical symptoms or realize, to their surprise, that they have come to dislike someone they interact with regularly. However, when they do become aware that something is wrong, they would rather think it through than cry about it. While some people enjoy a good cry to get things out of their systems, Aquarians resolve emotional issues by considering the situation from multiple perspectives and identifying potential solutions or new ways of thinking.

Extroverted

Aquarians are friendly and open to social approaches from a wide variety of people unless their ascendants are in more introverted signs such as Virgo, Scorpio, Capricorn, or Pisces. Most Aquarians are happy to interact and work with groups of people, and they are energized when discussing big, important issues and ideas with intelligent companions (though most Aquarians dislike small talk and other shallow forms of interaction).

Although generally outgoing, Aquarians prefer to socialize in a way that provides intellectual stimulation, so they enjoy games, political or scientific organizations, or hobby-based clubs. Being adventurous by nature, some also gravitate to groups that engage in exciting activities (for example, travel to less popular destinations or dangerous sports).

Because Aquarians are people-oriented, they tend to work well with groups, though these groups must be progressive or unusual in some way to capture an Aquarian's interest. Also, groups must be egalitarian, as Aquarians dislike authority and hierarchy, and most won't tolerate anyone trying to boss them around.

Generous

Aquarians tend to be very generous with their resources because they are both helpful and impractical by nature. They will loan or give things away in response to altruistic impulses without a thought for their financial futures. As a result of this generosity (along with a propensity for careless spending in general), they can end up in dire financial circumstances unless their ascendants are in more pragmatic signs such as Taurus, Cancer, Virgo, Scorpio, or Capricorn, which make Aquarians less careless and more practical.

Aquarians are also generous with their time when anyone needs help with something or just to talk things through. They are as likely to help strangers as those they know well, so many are drawn to volunteer work.

Humanitarian

Most Aquarians have a humanitarian streak that makes them want to do something for the world, so many volunteer their time for charities or engage in environmental or political activism. Once Aquarians choose a cause, they can become obsessive and fanatical, making it difficult to socialize with anyone who doesn't support it. However, this obsessive tendency enables them to make significant achievements on behalf of their chosen issue.

Idealistic

Aquarians are highly idealistic. They believe that even the worst people can be redeemed and the most intractable problems solved, and they expect the world (and their own lives) to improve steadily over time. They tend to see the best in people and assume that others are honest and good until proven otherwise. They give everyone a fair chance, so they are vulnerable to the manipulations of unscrupulous people.

Aquarians are often drawn into politics or charitable activities, and they can devote an enormous amount of time to their favorite causes, to the point where their entire lives are taken up with working toward positive change. However, this is a means by which Aquarians achieve fulfilment, so they don't resent the time and energy required to act on their ideals.

Imprudent

Aquarius is a sign that leaps before looking, chasing new, exciting opportunities with wild abandon, heedless of the consequences. Typical Aquarians are impulsive, incautious, and careless by nature. As a result, they may live chaotic lives, sliding into debt, offending people, or losing one thing after another through rash, impractical decision making unless there are more pragmatic forces in their natal zodiacs (for example, a Taurus, Cancer, Scorpio, Virgo, or Capricorn ascendant) to provide some stability.

Aquarians are not usually good at saving money or doing the boring domestic chores required to maintain a household, so they may live in a chronic state of financial trouble and allow their homes to become disaster areas. A major challenge for this sign is learning how to be cautious, pragmatic, and sensible in situations where these traits are required.

Independent

Aquarians are fiercely independent and quick to run away from anyone who tries to restrain them and force them to live in a particular way. Freedom is critical to their happiness, and relationships with clingy, jealous partners are usually doomed to failure. Aquarians rarely require others to prop them up emotionally during times of challenge or change, so they have trouble understanding those who need a lot of emotional support, and they are not suited to high-maintenance partnerships in general.

Aquarians are not needy or possessive. They demand the freedom to do their own thing, but are sufficiently fair-minded to grant the same freedom to their partners. They are happiest with friends and lovers who have their own hobbies and interests and don't expect to spend every moment together.

Innovative

There is a brilliant, futurist streak running through the Aquarian personality that underlies a capacity for innovation. Aquarians have flashes of insight that can lead to new inventions or progressive ways of doing things. However, they have difficulty distinguishing brilliant ideas from crazy ones, which can act as a barrier to achievement.

Aquarians tend to be ahead of their time and inclined to think about how things could be in the future rather than how they are now. Rather than wallowing in nostalgia, most have a realistic sense of the problems associated with the past and present, and they spend a lot of time thinking about what could be changed or invented to make the world a better place.

Intellectual

Aquarians are intellectually oriented, processing life as a series of thoughts rather than feelings most of the time. They require plenty of intellectual stimulation, so most love to read nonfiction or fiction that introduces clever, complicated concepts (many Aquarians are sci-fi fans). Aquarians also spend a lot of time discussing philosophy, psychology, science, or politics with anyone who can provide new insights into a topic of interest or present an intelligent, rational argument, providing an opportunity for debate.

Because Aquarians are intellectuals by nature, intelligence is usually their most valued quality in partners and friends, and a romantic partner who offers no intellectual challenge will rarely last long. Aquarians select their companions for their fascinating minds, with appearance, status, and wealth playing less of a role than they do for other signs.

Open-minded

Aquarians gravitate to anyone who can offer new ideas or a fresh perspective. They are sympathetic to those who are excluded, persecuted, or ostracized for their outsider views, and will give a fair hearing to even the most obscure or strange theories, which makes them vulnerable to becoming obsessive conspiracy theorists (unfortunately, some Aquarians have trouble distinguishing brilliant from crazy).

Aquarians are willing to stick up for unpopular viewpoints, so they can be fearless champions on behalf of those bringing important truths to light or rising up to free themselves from oppressors. However, they can also be taken in by crackpots whose ideas or demands are being ignored for good reason.

Because Aquarians are so open-minded, some enjoy playing devil's advocate as an intellectual exercise, taking on an unpopular perspective in a debate just for the pleasure of honing their argumentative skills. They enjoy giving their intellects a good workout with worthy opponents and their openness to other perspectives allows them to consider more than one side of an issue. Unless they become obsessive about a particular cause, they tend to be fair-minded and balanced in their assessments.

Optimistic

Most Aquarians are set to sunny side up unless their ascendants or moon signs bring some doom and gloom to their personalities. Naturally inclined toward optimism, Aquarians believe that everything will turn out well in the end. Even in the face of extreme hardship and surrounded by those who have succumbed to despair, they can maintain a positive outlook that is inspiring to others.

If Aquarians suffer a bout of depression, they usually rebound more quickly than most. As a future-oriented sign, Aquarius is less likely to wallow in present misery or memories of past suffering. The Aquarian propensity for optimism and futuristic outlook enables them to cope unusually well with stress and change.

Original

Aquarians are known for their originality, which inclines them to reflexively reject anything conventional. They march to the beat of a different drummer and couldn't care less what mainstream types think about their choices. As a result, some Aquarians adopt very unusual belief systems or lifestyles.

Aquarians can offer unique perspectives on life, the universe, and everything, which makes them great problem solvers who can help others find creative solutions to problems that cannot be solved with traditional methods. They enjoy finding their own ways of doing things, which although different from the mainstream, often work just as well or even better, so they tend to be originators of new trends rather than followers of existing ones.

Progressive

Most Aquarians have a progressive outlook on life, so they are less likely to be bigoted or obsessed with an idealized past. Instead, they look to the future, and most want to increase equality in the world rather than gaining an unfair advantage for themselves at the expense of others.

Aquarians tend to be socially tolerant in their political views, even if they swing in a more conservative direction in general. Aquarius is among the few change-loving signs of the zodiac, and Aquarians are often at the forefront of political movements that seek to transform the existing social order.

Rebellious

A fierce rebellious streak runs through the Aquarian personality. If you want to get Aquarians to do something, just tell them they can't. On the positive side, their drive to question established orders can manifest as a tendency to stick up for the underdog, protest injustice, and even work to overthrow oppressive governments and institutions. On the other hand, Aquarians can end up on the wrong side of the law if their rebelliousness and disrespect for authority and rules are taken to extremes. However, most will be content with protesting any authority they find unreasonable rather than turning to a life of crime.

Although Aquarians have a penchant for lifelong learning and will usually educate themselves by reading on their own, school can be challenging because they dislike conventional environments and have trouble submitting to authority. However, if an Aquarian's ascendant is in a less rebellious sign, the tendency to chafe against authority will be reduced, allowing the Aquarius to enjoy the intellectual opportunities school provides without feeling oppressed.

Restless

Aquarians have a very low boredom threshold. Their restless natures spur them on to fill their lives with activities, intellectual pursuits, and social interaction. Lacking sufficient intellectual stimulation and new experiences, they may completely overturn their lives, leaving behind relationships, homes, or even nations, along with anything else that feels restrictive, in their search for novelty, adventure, and meaning.

Aquarians dislike routine and predictability. When stuck in jobs or relationships that present no variation and challenge, they tend to wander off in search of more interesting environments. Aquarians fear boredom more than the unknown, so they will usually try something new rather than continuing on in a situation they find unfulfilling.

Sensation-seeking

Most Aquarians are risk takers, as they are not prone to anxiety and tend to be incautious by nature. They seek novelty and excitement and love to try new things, which can lead them into danger and increase the risk of injury and financial loss.

Aquarians are happiest when they can regularly have new experiences. If they incorporate these opportunities into their daily routines, they are less likely to grow so bored that they do something crazy to stir things up and destroy their lives in the process.

Stubborn

Because Aquarians are so open-minded in general, people are often surprised by how stubborn they can be once they latch onto an idea, belief, or cause. When Aquarians are in search mode, they are good at considering all options and perspectives, but once something grabs them, whether it is a person, an ideology, or an activity, they can be fiercely loyal, even in the face of evidence that a belief system is false or an individual or activity is harmful.

The Aquarian stubbornness arises largely from rebelliousness. The more others try to change Aquarian minds or deter them from courses of action, the more they resist and insist on doing things their own way.

Tactless

Aquarians have many fine qualities, but tact is not among them. They can be honest to the point of cruelty, not because they want to be cruel, but because they value the truth above all else. They want others to be honest with them, even if they don't like what they hear, and they grant others the same respect, even when diplomacy would be a kinder strategy.

Aquarians can damage friendships, create strife within families, and lose jobs because they make thoughtless statements rather than taking the time to consider the emotional impacts of their words. While not inclined to be malicious, they can upset others with their emotional obliviousness. However, an Aquarius whose ascendant or moon is in a more sensitive sign (for example, Cancer, Scorpio, or Pisces) or a more diplomatic sign (such as Libra or Capricorn) will be far more careful with other people's feelings than a typical Aquarius.

Unpredictable

Aquarians are unpredictable because they have a need to regularly shake things up if life becomes too bound by routine. This trait can be upsetting to family members, friends, and lovers who require stability and consistency, leading to clashes with close associates who dislike change. Aquarians do best with companions who either enjoy mixing things up on a regular basis or can provide sufficient interest and excitement so that they don't feel the need to wander off in search of new experiences.

Because Aquarians are so unpredictable, they may overturn their lives every few years, moving to a new faraway place, seeking an entirely different field of work, devoting themselves to a new cause, or adopting a new ideology. However, this tendency is reduced if they get plenty of intellectual stimulation and challenge from their careers, hobbies, and companions.

The Atypical Aquarius

The sun sign isn't the only element that influences personality. Aspects and planetary placements, particularly the moon sign and rising sign (ascendant), are also important. For example, an Aquarius with Taurus rising will be more stable and practical, and Pisces rising makes an Aquarius more sensitive and intuitive.

There are many websites that offer free chart calculation to determine the other planetary placements and aspects in your natal zodiac, which provide a more comprehensive personality profile. Reading the personality profiles for your sun sign, ascendant, and moon sign is recommended to develop a better understanding of your personality.

See Appendix 2 for information about other astrological influences on personality.

Chapter 2: Aquarius Love and Friendship Style

Aquarians have trouble relating to conventional people, and they tend to select their companions based on unusual criteria. They value intellectual prowess and uniqueness over physical appearance and other more shallow attributes when choosing friends and lovers, and most have companions who represent a broad range of ages and social groups or cultural backgrounds. Only intelligent, creative, and original companions can hold an Aquarian's attention indefinitely; relationships with more mainstream types usually have an expiry date.

The Aquarian's primary requirements for friends and lovers are that they be interesting and smart. When Aquarians find clever, unusual companions who meet their odd criteria, most are extremely loyal, whether those people are good for them or not. Ideal companions for Aquarians are progressive, open-minded, intellectual, unusual, easy going, not prone to jealousy, and not exceptionally sensitive.

Aquarians have an exaggerated need for freedom, which can be upsetting for more needy types. They are happiest with friends and lovers who are as independent as they are, and they don't do well with companions who require lots of attention or emotional support. When Aquarians become ensnared by clingy individuals, they look for the quickest escape route they can find from the relationship.

Aquarians will try almost anything once, and as a result, they often develop obscure interests, hobbies, and collections of things. They are more likely to establish friendships and romantic relationships with those who have equally eclectic and unusual tastes, and who can share their more atypical hobbies or introduce them to new (and unconventional) activities.

Because they have such low boredom thresholds, Aquarians don't like to establish routines and are rarely satisfied with ordinary activities. They are most compatible with friends and lovers who share their need for novelty and exploration, and who are comfortable with change.

Relationship strengths

Aquarians are generous to their friends and partners, willing to give time and money (though they have trouble providing emotional support because they don't always understand why others feel the way they do or how someone could benefit from a good cry). Because Aquarians are so fair-minded, they are inclined to help acquaintances or even strangers as well as close friends and lovers, which may bother more possessive types.

Aquarians are tolerant of the quirks, idiosyncrasies, and strange beliefs of others. Moreover, they are willing to stick up for unpopular viewpoints, ideologies, or individuals if they believe these outsider views have merit or a person is being unfairly persecuted, so they can be loyal, supportive friends to those who have been abandoned or rejected by others. They are also nonjudgmental, and will listen to the problems and personal views of their companions with an open mind, offering unique solutions and fresh perspectives.

Most Aquarians are even-tempered due to their intellectual approach to problem solving. Although they love a spirited debate, they are not inclined to be deliberately cruel, pick real fights about sensitive issues, or have angry meltdowns (unless their ascendants are in more volatile signs). As a result, they are usually pleasant to live with because their emotional detachment makes them easy going, tolerant, and not inclined to fits of temper. They are low-maintenance friends and lovers because they aren't inclined to demand attention and require less emotional support than most.

Typical Aquarians are neither jealous nor possessive, and they don't feel a need to control their partners. Independent by nature, they allow their companions the freedom to do their own thing as well.

Relationship challenges

Aquarians love new experiences, which can make their behavior erratic and unpredictable. If things grow too settled in their relationships, they may turn their lives upside down on a whim, leaving their devastated partners behind and possibly damaging their own lives in the process as well.

Aquarians also have a tendency to provide intellectual answers to emotional questions, which can be hurtful to more sensitive types. Those who seek a deep emotional connection may find Aquarians too detached or passionless for their tastes. However, jealous types will suffer even more intensely in relationships with Aquarians, who are not inclined to soothe their fears about unfaithfulness and loss, and may instead rebel against any sign of possessiveness by retreating psychologically or physically, making the insecure partner feel even more anxious.

Aquarians are also not known for their domesticity. When lovers try to impose conventional, safe, predictable lifestyles on their Aquarian partners, the relationship is usually doomed to failure.

Chapter 3: Aquarius Compatibility with Other Sun Signs

Note: There is more to astrological compatibility than sun signs alone. Other elements in a person's natal zodiac also play a role. Ascendants (rising signs), moon signs, and other planetary placements and aspects shape personality and affect compatibility. For example, a Capricorn with Leo rising will be more extroverted than a typical Capricorn, and a Taurus with Aries rising or moon in Sagittarius will be more compatible with Aquarius than a typical Taurus. For more information on other natal zodiac elements, see Appendix 2.

Aquarius + Aries

Compatibility tends to be high with this combination. Both signs are independent, progressive, individualistic, sociable, freedom-loving seekers of novelty and excitement. These two don't need to spend every moment together, so they don't tie one another down or make each other feel oppressed.

Aquarians have a number of traits that increase their compatibility with Aries. Although they love a good debate, unlike Aries, they aren't usually combative and are not inclined to dominate others, so they're unlikely to trigger a rebellious Aries backlash (which often occurs with more bossy or controlling types). Aquarians also tend to be tolerant and not emotionally reactive, so they're unlikely to become upset in response to Aries provocation. In addition, typical Aquarians are collaborative rather than competitive, so they don't compete directly with Aries, removing another potential source of conflict (the exception to this rule is an Aquarius with a feisty, aggressive rising sign such as Aries or Leo).

One potential problem with this match is that Aquarian emotional detachment may bother passionate, emotionally expressive Aries. Aries is a warm, affectionate fire sign whereas Aquarius is a cool, intellectually focused air sign. Aquarian detachment may make Aries feel insecure or even unloved at times, and this problem can be exacerbated by the Aquarian tendency to spend time with many different people and treat everyone similarly rather than prioritizing a romantic partner. Another problem with this match is that neither sign is particularly sensible, so the practical aspects of life may go unaddressed, leading to problems. However, this is otherwise an excellent pairing unless their ascendants and moon signs are not compatible.

Aquarius and Aries are likely to hold one another's interest for a number of reasons. Aquarius tends to be unpredictable and open to new experiences, so Aries is less likely to grow bored, and Aries is dynamic, impulsive, and also driven to seek new experiences, so Aquarius won't suffer a descent into stultifying routine. These two are unlikely to get into a rut because one or the other will promote change at the first sign of things becoming too settled. They keep things lively and interesting, which gives their match more sticking power. In a best-case scenario, Aries strength and decisiveness will have a stabilizing effect on erratic Aquarius, while Aquarius's tolerant, calm nature helps frenetic Aries become more peaceful and focused.

Aquarius + Taurus

This can be a difficult combination. Aquarius is a creature of the mind and Taurus is earthy and sensual. Tauruses experience the world through their senses and intuitions, whereas Aquarians tend to process their experiences intellectually and be detached from their emotions. Although the differences between these two signs can make their interactions interesting, they will usually have very different tastes and lifestyle preferences that make it difficult for them to live together.

Aquarians love change and seek it out, while Tauruses loathe and avoid it. If Aquarius manages to implement major life changes on a whim, Taurus will be distressed, but if Taurus keeps things consistent, Aquarius will grow bored. Stability-loving Taurus will find Aquarian unpredictability stressful, while Aquarius will find Taurean routines dull.

Social issues can be a significant point of contention with this sun sign combination. Tauruses like to spend time at home, in the homes of close friends, or out in nature (unless their ascendants fall in more gregarious signs), whereas the typical Aquarius wants to get out and meet new people in a wider variety of places.

Another problem with this match is that Aquarians are independent and fiercely protective of their freedom. They like to have friends and interests outside their primary relationships. However, the typical Taurus is possessive and may become jealous of an Aquarian's life outside the relationship and request more time together as a couple. If Aquarius refuses, Taurus may suffer from chronic feelings of insecurity. On the other hand, Aquarius may agree to these terms but feel trapped within the relationship.

Although these two signs are not very compatible, if a couple's ascendants or moon signs bring their temperaments into better alignment, this can be a positive match in which the two individuals balance each other out nicely (for example, an Aquarian with a Taurus, Cancer, or Capricorn ascendant is a better bet for Taurus, and a Taurus with an Aries, Gemini, Libra, Sagittarius, or Aquarius ascendant is a better prospect for Aquarius). When other aspects of their natal zodiacs are more compatible, these two disparate personalities can have positive effects on one another, with Aquarius encouraging Taurus to try new things and entertain new ideas, and Taurus helping Aquarius cultivate some much-needed stability and pragmatism. However, for this relationship to be successful, Aquarius will need to provide the reassurance and evidence of commitment

Taurus requires, and Taurus will have to allow Aquarius time and space for independent activities.

Aquarius + Gemini

This is a wonderful combination for compatibility. The intellectual rapport is excellent and these two individuals tend to get along well. In a romantic pairing, this may not be a very passionate or intense combination, though it should be intellectually stimulating and harmonious. Gemini and Aquarius may part ways to pursue other interests or because the romantic connection lacks depth, but it is more likely to be an amicable parting than a hostile one.

If these two live together or get married, their relationship will probably resemble a close friendship rather than a stormy romance. If they do clash, it is likely to occur because Aquarians tend to be straightforward and honest, whereas Geminis can be deceptive unless other elements in their natal zodiacs make them more forthright and direct. Some Geminis lie about important issues; others are simply creative, entertaining storytellers who embellish their tales to make them more interesting. However, this tendency can irritate Aquarians, who want the whole truth and nothing but the truth.

One of the most positive aspects of the Gemini-Aquarius match is that both individuals value their freedom and independence. Neither has a tendency to be jealous or possessive, so they don't hold one another back. Although they can have a lot of fun together, they can also have fun with other friends and pursue their own interests without upsetting each another. Also, both signs tend to become bored if things grow routine, so neither is likely to let this happen. Additional points in favor of this relationship are that Aquarius is better able to tolerate Gemini's changeability than those of most other signs, and Gemini is less likely to be bothered by Aquarius's emotional detachment. Both signs tend to be cerebral rather than emotional, so they are more likely to connect based on thoughts than feelings.

Both Gemini and Aquarius are full of surprises, which keeps things interesting. They welcome the unexpected and cope well with change. Conversations tend to be fascinating, and these two can expand one another's horizons, introducing each other to new ideas and experiences. Both tend to be curious and sociable, and they share a love of novelty that causes them to chase new experiences and ideologies (unfortunately, this can pull them apart if their interests diverge too much). The key to success for this match will be shared interests, friendships, and viewpoints. Gemini's views are more flexible than those of Aquarius (Aquarius tends have fixed opinions and be very stubborn about changing them), so Gemini is more likely to compromise.

Aquarians enjoy a good debate, but they are not inclined to get emotional about it, and although Geminis may stir things up a little from time to time, they don't usually start major battles within their relationships, so severe clashes between these two are unlikely. If fights do occur, both signs tend to get over things quickly because neither is particularly sensitive or prone to holding grudges. If Gemini and Aquarius do part ways, they are more likely to drift apart while remaining friends (or at least on friendly terms) than to burst apart in an explosion of mutual rage unless other elements in the two natal zodiacs are very incompatible.

Aquarius + Cancer

This is a difficult match unless other elements in the two natal zodiacs are highly compatible. The Aquarian emotional detachment will be distressing to Cancer, while Cancer's dependency and sensitivity will make Aquarius feel trapped. Cancer does better with a warmer, more affectionate companion, whereas Aquarius tends to be happier with a more independent and less sensitive lover or friend.

Cancer and Aquarius have very different relational styles and lifestyle preferences, which can make long-term relationships difficult. Cancers tend to be nurturing and sensitive to the needs of others. They usually want to stay close to their families, cultivate a small number of longstanding friendships, and remain in one place rather than moving around. Aquarians, on the other hand, get their intellectual stimulation through seeking new connections and experiences. They relate to others in a cerebral rather than an emotional way, and although most aren't deliberately cruel, they lack emotional intuition, so they may hurt the feelings of more sensitive types unintentionally. They are also independent by nature and require the freedom to pursue a variety of interests and maintain friendships outside of their primary relationships. Their fear of boredom also leads them to make sweeping life changes on a whim and spend money carelessly, both which are upsetting to security-conscious Cancers.

Cancers and Aquarians also tend to have different interests and outlooks on life. Cancers are sentimental and past-oriented, while Aquarians are futuristic and progressive. These differences influence their preferred pastimes, political leanings, and what they like to do with their free time. Cancers typically prefer home-based or outdoor pursuits and small gatherings of friends or family, whereas typical Aquarians are drawn to technology-based, political, or cultural activities and have a stronger need to make new connections. Whether they fall to the right or the left of the political spectrum, Cancers are inclined to be conventional in their political beliefs, whereas Aquarians often adopt more radical belief systems (typically on the left side of the spectrum, though they may also swing right, but in unusual ways).

In a romantic relationship, the typical Cancer wants to spend plenty of time alone with a partner. The typical Aquarius, by contrast, prefers to spend time among groups of friends and will be aggravated by Cancer's possessiveness. Cancer may find Aquarius cold and distant because Aquarius is unlikely to provide much in the way of romance, heartfelt discussion, and personal attention, while Aquarius is bewildered by Cancer's cycling moods and emotionally reactive nature. Cancer may take the Aquarian need for time apart as a rejection, while Aquarius perceives Cancer's need for regular reassurance as a character flaw.

The success of this challenging match will likely depend on Cancer's willingness to lower expectations regarding traditional romance and allow Aquarius more freedom, and Aquarius's willingness to soothe Cancer's insecurities with words and deeds when necessary. Both will need to compromise on a variety of issues (unless other elements in their natal zodiacs bring their temperaments into better alignment). In a best-case scenario, these two will meet each other halfway, with Aquarius picking up some of Cancer's pragmatism and common sense and Cancer absorbing some of the Aquarian optimism and self-protective emotional detachment.

Aquarius + Leo

This can be a difficult combination. Aquarians are more cerebral than physical, while Leos are very emotionally expressive and physically demonstrative. Leos need frequent assurances of love and attraction that Aquarians usually fail to provide. As a result, Leo may end up feeling unloved in this pairing, while Aquarius finds Leo overly needy. To make matters worse, Leos want the lion's share of their partners' attention, while Aquarians tend to divide their time equally among all those in their lives. Loyal Leos need special treatment to feel secure in a relationship, but fair-minded Aquarians tend to treat everyone they like similarly, which can create problems in a romantic relationship.

These two also tend to differ politically and in terms of preferred lifestyles, with Leos typically being more conventional and Aquarians gravitating toward unusual political views and lifestyle choices.

Another point of contention between these two signs is that Leos are appearance-conscious, while typical Aquarians have little interest in surface things. Aquarians are concerned with ideas and philosophies, so Leo's interest in clothing, social status, and glamorous events and people will seem shallow to

Aquarius, while many Aquarian pursuits (and friends) will seem eccentric or even crazy to Leo.

Aquarius wants lots of personal freedom and will probably find Leo too possessive and demanding, and Leo may find Aquarius cold and aloof. However, if other elements in their natal zodiacs are more compatible, this can be interesting match, and these two individuals may have positive effects on one another.

Leos can benefit from cultivating some Aquarian detachment to reduce their sensitivity to criticism, and they will expand their horizons by adopting a more open-minded Aquarian approach to life. Leos, in turn, can act as stabilizing forces for Aquarians, who are so open to new ideas that they may ruin their lives in the service of crackpot theories and ideologies (or even dangerous people in extreme cases). Both signs seek excitement and new experiences, so if they can overcome their differences, these two can have a lot of fun together, and the relationship is unlikely to ever grow dull.

Aquarius + Virgo

This can be challenging. Although both individuals live largely in their minds and can develop an intellectually stimulating rapport, it is unlikely that this relationship will go very deep unless the ascendants and moon signs of these two bring their temperaments into better alignment.

Connecting emotionally can be difficult for this pair. Virgo is cautious and slow to trust, and Aquarius is not particularly sensitive. Unless other elements in their natal zodiacs create more warmth, these two individuals may be emotionally distant from each other and the relationship may lack affection. On the plus side, Virgo is less likely than those of many other signs to be jealous of Aquarius's outside activities and interests, and Aquarius won't mind giving Virgo the freedom to pursue hobbies independently as well. However, these two may have difficulty living together.

Aquarian unpredictability will bother Virgo, and the typical Aquarius won't respect or even understand Virgo's need for consistency. Virgo craves security and can become very anxious in unstable situations, while Aquarius thrives on novelty and change. These conflicting tendencies create a situation in which these two are often at cross-purposes, and both will have to do a lot of compromising to make their relationship work. In a worst-case scenario, they will drift apart due to different lifestyle preferences.

In addition to their sharp intellects, Virgo and Aquarius often share a desire to serve humanity in some way, so they can forge productive partnerships for charitable or political aims, but they are likely to irritate one another in day-to-day life. However, when they pair up, the connection tends to be intellectually stimulating and mind expanding, so this can be an interesting match, but it will have more potential if these two have ascendants that bring their temperaments into better alignment (for example, a Virgo with Gemini, Libra, Sagittarius, or Aquarius rising is a better prospect for Aquarius, and an Aquarius with a Taurus, Cancer, Scorpio, or Capricorn ascendant will be more compatible with Virgo).

Ideally, Virgo and Aquarius will have positive effects on one another, with Virgo steering Aquarius toward a healthier and more productive lifestyle and Aquarius opening Virgo's mind to new ideas and experiences. If these two establish a business partnership, the Aquarian visionary streak combined with the Virgo work ethic and achievement orientation could produce great things, provided these two can manage to work together.

Aquarius + Libra

Libra and Aquarius usually get along well and understand one another on a deeper level. They enjoy a great intellectual rapport and should have a harmonious relationship because although both like to debate, neither is inclined toward fighting over emotionally charged issues unless their ascendants are in more combative signs. In fact, both prefer to live in their heads and process things rationally rather than through the distorting lens of feelings.

The rapport between Libra and Aquarius tends to be easy and laid back, which is great for day-to-day living, though this match may lack passion in a romantic relationship unless other elements in their natal zodiacs provide some sparks. However, the conversation should be great and these two are likely to share some interests, creating common ground over which to bond. If a deeper relationship develops, it is more likely to resemble a solid friendship with bedroom privileges than a stormy romance with an inevitable expiry date.

Both Libra and Aquarius tend to be quite sociable, but Aquarians are more inclined to use their social time productively by joining groups involved in charitable or political activities or working with others to do or produce something. This Aquarian activity-focused socializing can inspire Libra to take up new causes and activities as well. Libras, in turn, have the diplomatic skills required to gently steer Aquarians away from some of their more crazy or detrimental pursuits without being perceived as oppressive. This is important, because Aquarians are fiercely freedom-oriented and stubborn, and they resent those who tell them what to do. Libras are skilled at persuading others without making them feel as though they're being ordered about, which is a much-needed ability in a relationship with an Aquarius.

Libra and Aquarius will usually give one another the social freedom each requires, allowing for friendships and hobbies outside the primary romantic partnership. Libras are more relationship-oriented than Aquarians, who tend to spread their energies amongst a wider circle of people even when sexually faithful. However, this shouldn't be a deal breaker, as Libras are very good at understanding and accommodating other people's perspectives and allowing them the space they need to pursue their own interests. Overall this is a highly compatible match for friendship and romance.

Aquarius + Scorpio

This is a problematic match unless other elements in the two natal zodiacs are more compatible. Scorpio and Aquarius have vastly different needs and lifestyle preferences. Typical Aquarians prefer to spend their time with groups of people rather than alone with a partner and they require a lot of personal freedom, which conflicts with the Scorpio need for visible commitment and security in a relationship. To make matters worse, Aquarian emotional detachment can be frustrating for passionate Scorpio. Because they have such different approaches to life, these two may have difficulty getting along day to day.

Typical Scorpios need to maintain control within their relationships to feel secure, while Aquarians require purely egalitarian connections. Aquarians also tend to have a lot of interests outside their relationships, and the time Aquarius spends engaging in activities with others can trigger Scorpio's jealousy. In addition, Aquarians can be emotionally oblivious, hurting the feelings of those they care about without meaning to. This problem arises because they tend to think about things rather than feeling them. They don't usually get upset over things that distress more sensitive signs, and

Scorpio finds Aquarius's calm detachment in response to important issues maddening.

Ultimately, it will be difficult for these two to understand one another and agree on almost any issue, and this disconnection can lead to stressful and bewildering interactions. However, these signs usually do share a few interests in common, typically those outside the mainstream, so there can be some common ground over which to bond. Both also cope well with change. However, lifestyle preferences are likely to be poles apart.

Scorpios tend to be lone wolves. They usually prefer to work alone, engage in solo hobbies or those that can be done with small groups of close friends or a partner, and generally maintain their privacy. Aquarians, by contrast, prefer to work and play among diverse groups of people. They are better able to let things go, so they tend to be less committed to homes, activities, and even people in some cases. The typical Aquarius can happily pick up and move on to a new place and make friends easily, but this is far more difficult for Scorpios, who are slow to trust and want to forge deeper, long-term bonds.

For the Scorpio-Aquarius pairing to work, these two will need to meet each other halfway. Scorpio will have to allow Aquarius more social freedom without harboring any resentment about it, and Aquarius will need to provide reassurance and demonstrate commitment by spending more quality time alone with Scorpio. These two will probably find each other's minds fascinating, and if they can compromise on the issues that divide them, this can be an interesting and intellectually stimulating match. Compatibility will be higher if their ascendants bring their temperaments and lifestyle preferences into better alignment.

Aquarius + Sagittarius

These two signs are very compatible. Both are open-minded, sociable, experimental, freedom loving, rebellious, and not particularly sensitive. Forthright Sagittarius is less likely to hurt Aquarius's feelings than those of many other signs because Aquarians are not quick to take offense. Also, both signs tend to be independent, so neither is likely to be clingy. They are also typically forward-thinking, visionary, intellectual, and somewhat eccentric, so this can be an intellectually stimulating and mind-expanding match. However, in romance, it may not be exceptionally passionate unless other elements in their natal zodiacs add some sparks.

The intellectual rapport is great with this pairing, and conversations should be endlessly fascinating. Both signs tend to be comfortable with change and inclined to seek new experiences, and they share a common restlessness that can lead them to go off adventuring together. They will introduce each other to new things and broaden one another's horizons, which helps to hold their mutual interest. However, neither is particularly sentimental, so the relationship may lack emotional depth and be more a meeting of the minds or a cheerful friendship with benefits than a passionate romance unless these individuals have their ascendants or moons in water signs (Cancer, Scorpio, or Pisces).

Sagittarius and Aquarius understand one another's needs for space and independence, so neither gets upset if the other pursues interests outside the relationship. If this casual attitude is taken to the extreme, these two may drift apart even if they get along well because their emotional connection is shallow and their outside interests pull them in new directions. Neither is particularly domestic either, as both tend to place a much higher value on experiences than material belongings and home bases, so it's easy for them to drift from one place to another without too much fuss (and to get into financial troubles along the way).

If these two do settle down within a romantic relationship, they are likely to be good friends as well as lovers, and to keep one another's interest alive. This tends to be a quirky, idealistic, fun match. However, this pair can get into difficulties because both individuals are impractical sensation seekers and rebels by nature, so neither partner puts any restraint on the other. These two will need to keep a close eye on their finances and the other mundane details of life to avoid problems later on.

Aquarius + Capricorn

This can be a difficult match. The infamous Aquarian unpredictability may distress Capricorn, and Capricorn's conventionality and caution will clash with Aquarius's eccentricity and experimental nature. Also, these two might have trouble establishing a deeper connection because both have a tendency to be emotionally detached. On the other hand, this can be beneficial because neither will expect romantic words and gestures or long discussions about feelings that the other is unlikely to provide.

The Capricorn dignity and self-discipline (which can tip over into self-denial and self-censorship) is at odds with the Aquarian penchant for self-expression (which can become crackpot radicalism in extreme individuals). Aquarians are natural rebels and contrarians, even when the contrary view is wrong or there is nothing to rebel against, while Capricorns often cling to habit or tradition, even when it brings unhappiness and should be discarded. Typical Capricorns also like to establish a solid home base and make it as nice as possible, and to work their way up within a single career field, whereas Aquarians are more likely to bounce from place to place and career to career because they are driven to seek change, particularly in times of stress. Capricorns, by contrast, crave security and stability when under pressure. These differences can lead to a variety of problems for this pair.

On the plus side, these two can be a nice complement to one another. Capricorn can take care of the practical side of life and keep Aquarius from doing anything too crazy that will cause regret later on, and Aquarius can help Capricorn break free of dull routines and get out and socialize more frequently (Capricorns have a tendency to isolate themselves, pursuing work-related projects, hobbies, and health interests at the expense of their social lives). Aquarius's buoyant optimism can also have a positive effect on Capricorn, countering a tendency toward depressiveness, while Capricorn's realism will help Aquarius avoid the pitfalls of crazy schemes and nutty or unscrupulous people (Aquarians are trusting by nature and easily led astray, so they can find themselves under the influence of harmful groups and individuals; Capricorns are good at spotting and avoiding these types).

A Capricorn-Aquarius romantic pairing may not be very affectionate, but its friendship component is likely to be strong and solid. If Aquarius can settle down and stay put and Capricorn can become a little more open-minded and venturesome, this match has potential, though much will depend on the compatibility of other elements in their natal zodiacs.

Aquarius + Aquarius

This is a great combination. The intellectual rapport is excellent and compatibility is high. Two Aquarians will respect one another's independence. They don't need to spend every moment together, and they are happy to allow each other the freedom to pursue hobbies and friendships outside their primary relationship. Neither is likely to be demanding or prone to insecurity, so these two shouldn't weigh each other down with neediness.

Aquarians have a broad range of interests, but even if their interests don't overlap, this won't matter too much with this pairing. These two should get along well in day-to-day life. Both enjoy a good debate, but neither is prone to fighting unless their ascendants fall in scrappier signs. They can have plenty of fascinating discussions, and because they have outside interests and are drawn to the unusual, they will never run out of interesting new things to talk about. Given their sociable and humanitarian natures, two Aquarians may be drawn to the same social or charitable causes, political movements, or other group activities aimed at changing the world for the better, which provides an opportunity for bonding over shared passions.

Aquarians are not particularly domestic or house-proud, so if they live together, their place of residence may be simply a place to sleep, hang out with friends, and store belongings. Aquarians have a tendency to gather eclectic assortments of stuff, so their homes can become a chaos of random objects stored in unexpected places (or strewn across every available surface). Aquarians usually keep housework to a minimum because they're more interested in ideas and experiences than the appearance of the material world around them.

Aquarians tend to process things rationally rather than emotionally, so although both individuals are quite forthright (even to the point of rudeness at times), neither is likely to do significant long-term damage to the other's feelings. This mutual emotional detachment means that even romantic partnerships can be more like friendships than love affairs with this pair. However, this is not necessarily a bad thing because friendship is a better basis for long-term commitment than the torrid emotional roller coaster of a passionate romance.

Aquarians are not the most practical individuals, and two Aquarians will not stand in the way of each other's more risky or ill-advised pursuits. They can also keep such a light hold on one another that they drift apart.

However, an Aquarius-Aquarius match has a higher-than-average likelihood of lasting, and when two Aquarians do part ways, it's more likely to happen because different interests have pulled them in new directions rather than the result of vicious battles or cold stalemates, so breakups between these two tend to be friendlier than those occurring with more combustible sun-sign pairings.

Aquarius + Pisces

Pisceans tend to be unusual in some way, which fascinates Aquarius, and Pisces finds Aquarian unconventionality and innovativeness appealing as well, so these two are often drawn to each other.

Both Aquarius and Pisces tend to see the world in grand, sweeping terms. They are idealistic sensation-seekers, so neither can act as an anchor for the other. This combination ensures a very interesting meeting of the minds, but there are a number of significant differences in how these two signs interact with the world that can create problems in a serious relationship.

Although both signs have a tendency toward altruism, Pisces is typically the more compassionate of the two. Aquarius has humanitarian ideals, but thinks in terms of changing the world to make it better for many people (or all of them) rather than ministering to the emotional needs of individuals. Pisceans are very sensitive, both to the feelings of others and on their own behalf. Pisces is easily hurt by careless statements, which emotionally oblivious Aquarius is prone to making, so there is the potential for emotional damage here. On the other hand, both signs tend to be tolerant and nonjudgmental, which reduces the risk of conflicts and allows both members of this pair to be themselves without fear of censure.

Another challenge with this combination is that Aquarius needs a lot of personal freedom, whereas Pisces requires plenty of reassurance (and comforting when bleak moods strike). Aquarius may find Pisces needy or overly emotional (which will send Aquarius packing), and Pisces may find Aquarius devastatingly cold and distant (which will send Pisces off in search of a more sympathetic partner).

Aquarians tend to spread their energies among many different people, treating friends and lovers similarly, but Pisceans need to feel that they are being prioritized by their partners. Typical Pisceans also want to rescue someone else or be rescued (depending on other personality factors) and independent Aquarius is not inclined to fulfill either of these roles, so Pisces may wander off in search of someone who is more needy or has a desire to take care of others. To make matters worse, neither sign tends to be particularly stable in terms of emotions or lifestyle, so they can't provide stability for each other unless their ascendants are in more solid signs such as Taurus, Cancer, Leo, Scorpio, or Capricorn.

In a best-case scenario, these two will learn from each other. Pisces can benefit from developing more rationality and a thicker skin, and Aquarius could improve relationships with others by cultivating Piscean strengths such as intuition and sensitivity. Both individuals are prone to streaks of brilliance, so they can come up with fascinating new ideas and insights, and if they work together, they can harness great collective potential for creativity and innovation. However, although this match does have some positive elements, these two will need to compromise on a number of issues. In particular, Aquarius will have to provide more affection and reassurance than is typical for this sign, as well as showing more restraint when broaching sensitive issues, and Pisces must allow Aquarius to pursue friendships and activities outside of the primary relationship.

Chapter 4: Aquarius Marriage and Divorce

Traditional astrological wisdom holds that Aquarians are most compatible with Aries, Gemini, Libra, Sagittarius, and Aquarius, and least compatible with Taurus, Cancer, Leo, Virgo, Scorpio, and Capricorn, but what do the actual marriage and divorce statistics say?

Mathematician Gunter Sachs (1998) conducted a large-scale study of sun signs, encompassing nearly one million people in Switzerland, which found statistically significant results on a number of measures, including marriage and divorce. Castille (2000) conducted a similar study in France using marriage statistics collected between 1976 and 1997, which included more than six million marriages. On the following pages, sun sign marriage pairings with Aquarius men and women are ranked from most to least common based on the findings of these studies (*indicates that a result is statistically significant—in other words, the marriage rate was much higher or lower than would occur by random chance).

Aquarius Men

Sachs Study

1. Aquarius*
2. Leo
3. Gemini
4. Virgo
5. Capricorn
6. Pisces
7. Sagittarius
8. Aries
9. Libra
10. Cancer
11. Scorpio*
12. Taurus*

Castille Study

1. Aquarius*
2. Taurus
3. Cancer
4. Pisces
5. Sagittarius
6. Capricorn
7. Gemini
8. Aries
9. Libra
10. Scorpio
11. Leo*
12. Virgo*

Aquarius Women

Sachs Study

1. Aquarius*
2. Pisces
3. Cancer
4. Capricorn
5. Sagittarius
6. Scorpio
7. Gemini
8. Libra
9. Taurus
10. Aries
11. Virgo
12. Leo*

Castille Study

1. Aquarius*
2. Capricorn
3. Sagittarius
4. Cancer
5. Leo
6. Aries
7. Pisces
8. Gemini
9. Taurus
10. Libra
11. Virgo
12. Scorpio

Some Notes on Marriage Rates

It's no surprise to see Aquarius topping the list in both studies. Two Aquarians are likely to have shared interests, tolerate one another's quirks and idiosyncrasies, and give each another plenty of personal freedom. Although Aquarians can be naturally contrary because they enjoy the intellectual stimulation of a good debate, most are not inclined to engage in damaging emotional arguments.

It's also unsurprising that Aquarius men marry Taurus and Scorpio women less often than those of other signs, according to the Sachs study. Tauruses and Scorpios can be prone to jealousy, and Aquarians, who value their independence, may find them too possessive.

There are no surprises at the bottom of the men's marriage list in the Castille study either, with lower rates of marriage between Aquarius men and Virgo and Leo women.

Although Virgo and Aquarius may develop an intellectual rapport, they tend to have different lifestyle preferences. Typical Aquarians are interested in culture, ideas, science, or other topics that could be considered people-oriented or technology-oriented, whereas typical Virgos are usually drawn toward health, fitness, nutrition, environmentalism, and other naturalistic fields. Also, Aquarians are open to unusual ideas and theories, whereas Virgos tend to seek irrefutable proof before they will entertain new perspectives. In addition, Aquarians tend to be quite extroverted, while Virgos are naturally introverted (though a Virgo whose ascendant is in an air or fire sign will probably be more sociable).

As for Leo and Aquarius, there are a number of reasons why this pairing may be difficult. Leo is a sign of the heart, and Aquarius a sign of the mind. Typical Leos also love material things, whereas Aquarians are drawn to ideas and the intangible aspects of life. Leos seek affluence, while Aquarians are usually less interested in this (or in some cases, almost completely indifferent to the material world). Leos require lots of personal attention, whereas Aquarians tend to spread their energies across diverse groups of people. Typical Leos also prefer a partner with a sense of style, and Aquarians are normally oblivious to fashion, except perhaps for the occasional quirky fad. Leos are fiery and passionate by nature, whereas Aquarians tend to be emotionally detached, intellectually oriented, and so laid back and tolerant that others may view them as cold or indifferent.

Leo also took the bottom marriage slot for Aquarius women in the Sachs study. It may be particularly hard for Leo men to grant Aquarius women the freedom they require, given that Leos like to protect and care for others and may become unhappy if they don't feel needed by independent Aquarians.

However, despite the differences that make it challenging for Aquarians to get along with Virgos or Leos, if the couple's rising or moon signs are more compatible they could potentially make an interesting, lively match.

Divorce

The Sachs study also provides insights into which romantic matches are most likely to stick. The following are statistically significant findings for divorce rates (in other words, effects too big to attribute to random chance).

Note: Even if your partnership falls into one of the higher-than-average divorce rate categories, that doesn't mean it's doomed to failure. The sun sign is only one element in a natal zodiac that determines compatibility, and there may be other elements in your natal zodiacs that make you far more compatible than would be expected based on sun signs alone.

Aquarius Men

Most likely to divorce: Gemini and Cancer

Least likely to divorce: Aries and Leo

Aquarius men part ways most frequently with Gemini and Cancer women, but are least likely to divorce Aries and Leo.

Cancer and Aquarius are not usually a good match for compatibility, given that the typical Cancer requires sensitivity, romance, emotional support, lots of affection, and relationship security, whereas the typical Aquarian is emotionally detached, independent by nature, and likely to find an escape route if he feels that his partner is too needy.

Gemini and Aquarius, on the other hand, are considered a compatible match, so the higher-than-average divorce rate may be attributable to a lack of sticking power rather than incompatibility. Because both signs are impulsive, easily bored, and drawn to new people and situations, relationships may end because one or both wander off in search of something new or they are pulled in different directions by diverging interests.

As for the matches that are more likely to stick, Aries and Aquarius share a number of traits, including honesty, generosity, extroversion, political interest and/or activism, a need for excitement, and the desire to try new things on a regular basis, so they have a better-than-average likelihood of holding each other's interest.

Leo and Aquarius, by contrast, are supposedly incompatible, but they do share some important traits, including sociability, generosity, forthrightness, and the desire for exciting new experiences, which may be the foundation for some of the longer-lasting matches. While these two may not have the smoothest relationship, it will never be boring.

Aquarius Women

Most likely to divorce: No statistically significant finding for any sign

Least likely to divorce: Sagittarius

Aquarian women are less likely to divorce Sagittarians than those of any other sign, but they are not more likely to divorce any particular sign.

Matches between Aquarius and Sagittarius may be favored because neither is possessive and both tend to be extroverted, so they can enjoy a good social life together. Also, both signs are usually interested in either social or political causes and enjoy philosophical debate, and they will be tolerant of one other's quirks and idiosyncrasies.

The Aquarius-Sagittarius partnership tends to be low maintenance and easy, unless other elements in the two natal zodiacs are very incompatible. These two signs spur one another on to new adventures and experiences, and allow each other the space and freedom required to try new things, spend time with new people, and have their own hobbies and interests, so neither feels oppressed or bored within the relationship.

The Best Romantic Match for Aquarius

The best match for Aquarius appears to be another Aquarius and perhaps Sagittarius. However, Aquarians who find themselves romantically entangled with one of the less compatible signs shouldn't despair. Plenty of marriages between supposedly incompatible signs have lasted.

It's important to keep in mind that these are statistical tendencies; this doesn't mean that every romance between incompatible signs is doomed. For example, out of 6,498,320 marriages encompassing all possible sign combinations in the Castille study, there were 1,059 *more* marriages between Aquarius men and Aquarius women than would be expected if sun signs had no effect, whereas between Aquarius men and Virgo women, there were 529 *fewer* marriages than would be expected if pairings were random. However, there still were many marriages between the supposedly least compatible signs.

Astrology is complex, and there is more to take into account than just sun signs. Two people with incompatible sun signs may have highly compatible rising signs or moon signs that can make the difference between a bad match and a good match with a bit of an "edge" that keeps things interesting.

*The Sachs study has been criticized for not taking potential confounding variables into account and continues to be controversial. I have found no critiques of the Castille study thus far.

Chapter 5: Why Some Signs Are More Compatible with Aquarius Than Others

Why are some astrological signs considered more or less compatible with Aquarius than others? Traditional astrologers believe that signs of the same element will be the most compatible, and that fire and air signs will be more compatible with one another, as will earth and water signs, whereas fire and air are more likely to clash with earth and water. They also believe that clashes are more likely to occur among different signs of the same quality (cardinal, fixed, or mutable).

Compatibility according to traditional astrologers:

- Aquarius (air, fixed) + Aries (fire, cardinal): good

- Aquarius (air, fixed) + Taurus (earth, fixed): very challenging

- Aquarius (air, fixed) + Gemini (air, mutable): excellent

- Aquarius (air, fixed) + Cancer (water, cardinal): very challenging

- Aquarius (air, fixed) + Leo (fire, fixed): very challenging

- Aquarius (air, fixed) + Virgo (earth, mutable): somewhat challenging

- Aquarius (air, fixed) + Libra (air, cardinal): excellent

- Aquarius (air, fixed) + Scorpio (water, fixed): very challenging

- Aquarius (air, fixed) + Sagittarius (fire, mutable): good

- Aquarius (air, fixed) + Capricorn (earth, cardinal): somewhat challenging

- Aquarius (air, fixed) + Aquarius (air, fixed): excellent

- Aquarius (air, fixed) + Pisces (water, mutable): somewhat challenging

Note: Two people who seem incompatible based on their sun signs may actually be far more compatible than expected because the elements and qualities of other placements in their natal zodiacs (ascendants, moon signs, etc.) are a much better match. See Appendix 2 for more information on this.

The Elements

The astrological elements are fire, earth, air, and water. Each element includes three of the twelve astrological signs.

Fire Signs: Aries, Leo, Sagittarius

Those who have a lot of planets in fire signs tend to be courageous, enterprising, and confident. Their love of excitement causes them take risks, and they are often extravagant or careless with money.

Fire people are generous to a fault, idealistic, and helpful. They are quick to anger, but also quick to forgive, and usually honest, in many cases to the point of bluntness or tactlessness.

Fire people are energetic and often athletic. They are assertive and in some cases aggressive or argumentative. Impulsivity can lead to poor decisions, financial disasters, and unnecessary conflict. Extroverted and easily bored, they seek attention and tend to be affectionate and friendly.

Earth Signs: Taurus, Virgo, Capricorn

Those who have many planets in earth signs tend to be responsible, reliable, and trustworthy. They can usually be counted on to provide stability and practical help, and they are loyal to their friends and not inclined to be fickle, though when someone crosses them, they can be quite ruthless in cutting that person out of their lives forever. Sane, reasonable, and diplomatic, those whose charts are weighted toward earth are slow to anger but also slow to forgive, and often hold grudges. However, they are usually reasonable and diplomatic unless severely provoked.

Those with a preponderance of earth signs in their charts tend to be physically strong and have great endurance. They are inclined to achieve success through hard work, and their innate cautiousness, fear of change, and need for security keep them from making rash decisions or gambling excessively, though these traits can also cause them to miss opportunities or get into ruts. While not exceptionally innovative, they have good follow-through and are able to finish what they start.

Air Signs: Gemini, Libra, Aquarius

Those who have a lot of planets in air signs tend to be intellectual in outlook rather than emotional, which can cause some to view them as insensitive. Logical, rational, and emotionally detached by nature, they can be open-minded and non-judgmental in most cases. Air people also tend to be friendly and sociable.

Air sign people are adaptable, mentally flexible, and easy going. They tend not to blow up at others in anger-provoking situations, as they are more inclined to analyze circumstances than to react passionately. They are also easily bored and require a diverse array of social companions, hobbies, and other entertainments. Air people usually love change and tend to be experimental and open to new experiences. Impulsivity and curiosity often lead them to make impractical decisions or squander their money.

Water Signs: Cancer, Scorpio, Pisces

Those who have many planets in water signs are highly intuitive and therefore able to discern the emotions, needs, and motivations of others. Water people are compassionate and inclined to care for the physically sick and the emotionally damaged. They can be very self-sacrificing on behalf of those they care for, and even in the service of strangers in some cases.

Sensitive and easily hurt, water people often develop a tough outer shell to hide their vulnerability. They are passionate in their attachments to people and prone to jealousy. Because they are idealistic, they are also inclined to gloss over the faults of others, and as a result, they can be deceived by unscrupulous people.

Water people are sensual and creative. Given the right environment and opportunity, they can produce art, music, literature, or in some cases, inventions or scientific ideas that have profound effects on others.

The Qualities

The astrological qualities are fixed, cardinal, and mutable. Each category includes four of the astrological signs.

Cardinal: Aries, Cancer, Libra, Capricorn

A person with the majority of natal planets in cardinal signs will be enterprising and inclined to initiate courses of action. Cardinal people make things happen and transform situations. This can be done to the benefit or detriment of others.

Fixed: Taurus, Leo, Scorpio, Aquarius

Those who have a lot of planets in fixed signs have good follow-through. They tend to stick to a single course of action and carry out activities to their completion or conclusion. Fixed-sign people are often moody or stubborn, and they often have intense reactions to things. However, they can act as stabilizing forces for others because they tend to behave in a consistent manner.

Mutable: Gemini, Virgo, Sagittarius, Pisces

Those who have the majority of their planets in mutable signs are flexible and adaptable. They accept change and adjust well to new circumstances that can throw other types off kilter. Mutable people are often better in a crisis than in a stable situation.

See Appendix 2 for information on how to find your other planetary placements to determine which elements and qualities are predominant in your natal zodiac.

Chapter 6: Aquarius Children

Aquarian children can be rebellious and argumentative unless there are softening influences in their natal zodiacs (for example, a Libra ascendant or moon sign). They are stubborn by nature, and it is difficult to dissuade them from a course of action or impose restrictions on them. However, on the plus side, they tend to be easygoing, tolerant, helpful, good-natured, and rarely oversensitive or whiny.

Aquarian children tend to learn quickly, and many have an affinity for science, technology, engineering, or anything else that requires visual-spatial skills. They pick up new concepts quickly and may take things apart to figure out how they work (their desire to understand how things work may also manifest as an early interest in psychology).

Despite their love of learning, Aquarian children are particularly susceptible to boredom in mainstream classrooms. They do better in progressive educational settings where the focus is on group learning, experiential learning, discussion, and debate rather than reading textbooks and answering questions.

Many Aquarian children prefer unusual toys or anything electrical or battery powered. Good toys for Aquarian children include LEGO, building blocks, science play sets, craft supplies (particularly for artistic projects that involve the creation of patterns), remote-controlled airplanes or drones, and other gadgets.

Chapter 7: Aquarius Parents

Aquarius parents tend to be progressive, open-minded, and unconventional. They allow their children plenty of freedom to try new things and even take some risks, with the understanding that this is required for children to learn about the world and develop self-confidence. Aquarian parents are not inclined to be fussy or overprotective. Instead, the typical Aquarius has a relaxed attitude toward parenting.

Aquarians are naturally sociable, and they need to spend plenty of time interacting with other adults even after having children. Some may join parents' groups, but others will simply ensure that they make time to see their old friends no matter how busy they are. Making time for adult interaction is important for Aquarians because they have low boredom thresholds, and without the intellectual stimulation of adult conversation, they will be unfulfilled and unhappy.

Typical Aquarius parents are open-minded and nonjudgmental, so they are not oppressive or domineering unless their ascendants are in more controlling signs. They give their children an unusual amount of freedom and independence, and continue to pursue their own interests even after having children rather than sacrificing themselves and becoming bitter about lost opportunities.

Because Aquarians are intellectually oriented, they enjoy discussing issues and ideas with their kids, and they're not inclined to talk down to them. Instead, they talk up, introducing complicated concepts and big ideas to promote their children's intellectual growth, and they enjoy discovering how their kids perceive and understand the world. Aquarian parents are not inclined to force their beliefs on others, so they allow their children to make up their own minds about things.

The best Aquarian parents are easy going without being too lax and tolerant without spoiling their children. They ensure that their kids have lots of new experiences (and in many cases, opportunities to see or try unusual things), and because they are not inclined to be anxious or depressive, they rarely inflict negative states on their children. Instead, they radiate positivity, and their cheerfulness is infectious, instilling a sense of optimism in their kids that manifests as self-efficacy and a belief that the world is basically good. On the other hand, Aquarians at their worst can have such a light approach to parenting that they're barely there, prioritizing their own interests and enjoyments completely and refusing to do the mundane domestic tasks associated with parenthood. Some may even abandon their families completely to pursue more exciting prospects. Whether the best or the worst side of the Aquarian personality dominates in parenthood will depend on other influences in the natal zodiac.

Chapter 8: Aquarius Health and Safety

Aquarians have a tendency to neglect the most basic needs of their bodies (including food and sleep) because they don't want to miss out on anything interesting. They live so completely within their minds that nurturing their bodies can be an afterthought. As a result, they can suffer from exhaustion or malnourishment in extreme cases.

Aquarians are naturally stubborn, so it is difficult for them to slow down and take it easy. They can keep going for some time before they get run down because they are able to ignore bodily distress signals, and they are shocked and miserable when their bodies inevitably fail them after a great amount of abuse. Although Aquarians tend to be even-tempered (unless their ascendants are in more volatile signs), illness is one of the few things that can make them crabby or depressive.

Aquarians may suffer more than their fair share of illness because they skimp on sleep and other bodily needs, which has a negative effect on their immune systems. A major health challenge for this sign is getting enough sleep and engaging in other self-care behaviors, even if this means missing out on experiences.

Aquarians are sensation seekers, which also puts them at risk for substance abuse. Although this sign is not prone to addiction in general (unless the ascendant is in a more addictive sign such as Pisces or Sagittarius), most Aquarians don't know when to stop doing something, which can lead to addiction, illness, or injury.

Aquarians don't usually express their anger (or even overtly acknowledge it), and unexpressed rage or sadness can manifest as accident-proneness or muscle tension. For Aquarians, acknowledging and dealing with their deeper feelings can be a real challenge, but doing so can help to reduce the risk of accidents and physical ailments.

Chapter 9: Aquarius Hobbies

Pastimes associated with the sign of Aquarius include:

- activism
- anthropological studies
- astronomy
- collecting unusual things
- computer programming
- cycling
- hanging out in coffee shops or restaurants
- humanitarian or volunteer work
- intellectual and political debates
- inventing things or coming up with new ways of doing things

- paranormal (especially UFO) or occult studies
- playing with gadgets
- playing videogames
- reading (especially books on philosophy, politics, conspiracy theories, science fiction, fantasy, or occult topics, as well as comic books and graphic novels)
- scientific studies
- skiing and other individual sports (particularly snow sports)
- socializing
- traveling
- watching sci-fi or fantasy movies

Chapter 10: Aquarius Careers

Air signs are not suited to solitary or repetitive work. The best jobs for Aquarius involve a wide variety of tasks or responsibilities, new experiences, and social interaction.

Aquarians usually prefer working with groups rather than in isolation (an Aquarian freelancer will often choose to work in cafes or other shared spaces rather than alone at home). The air signs also tend to be open to adopting new technologies, so they are suited to technology-oriented professions.

Aquarians grow bored more quickly than most in traditional 9-5 jobs. Although not suited to working alone, they tend to have difficulty with authority, so they do best as part of an egalitarian group rather than a hierarchical structure. The ideal Aquarian job provides flexibility and the opportunity to labor on behalf of a good cause.

Aquarians can't tolerate being bossed around (even by a boss), which makes traditional work settings challenging for them, particularly if they get stuck with draconian supervisors. Typical Aquarians are more inclined to choose interesting careers than well-paid ones. Unusual and intellectually stimulating careers are best for this sign, though some are drawn to certain athletic pursuits as well, and many have a particular affinity for snow and ice sports and cycling.

Research conducted by Gunter Sachs found that Aquarians are more likely to be self-employed and less likely to be found in executive positions than those of other signs. This is unsurprising, given that Aquarians are fiercely independent, inclined to rebel against authority, opposed to hierarchical arrangements, and ill-suited to conventional employment.

Careers and career fields associated with the sign of Aquarius include:

- activist
- anthropologist
- architect
- astronaut
- astronomer
- athlete (particularly snow sports or cycling)
- charity or humanitarian worker
- comic book writer
- computer games developer
- computer programmer
- engineer
- inventor
- lawyer
- Peace Corps worker
- pilot
- politician
- professor/teacher
- psychologist
- reformer (law or politics)
- science fiction writer
- scientist (especially physics)
- social worker
- sociologist

Note: The sun sign is only one element within an astrological profile. Many other factors play a role, including rising and moon signs. For example, a person with the sun in Aquarius and Capricorn rising will be better able to manage in the 9-5 business world than a typical Aquarius.

Chapter 11: Aquarius Differences

Sachs collected a large volume of market research data for his study, and this data showed some average differences among the sun signs for certain beliefs, attitudes, interests, hobbies, activities, and preferences. The following are items for which there was a significant difference between Aquarius and the sun sign average (a significantly higher or lower percentage of positive or negative responses from Aquarians compared to the average for all the sun signs). Not all Aquarians followed these trends; they were just more likely to match them than those of other sun signs.

Housework

Aquarians were less likely to rate neatness and cleanliness as especially important in their lives. This is unsurprising, as Aquarians are not known for their tidiness or organizational skills.

Gender roles

Aquarius women were more likely to describe their attitudes, views, and inclinations as androgynous (as opposed to fulfilling a traditionally feminine gender role). This is also unsurprising, as typical Aquarians don't adhere to conventional stereotypes.

Relationships

Aquarius men and women were less likely to be single than those of other signs. This indicates that although Aquarians value their independence, they prefer to stick with their partnerships when they find companions who meet their unusual standards.

Decision making

Aquarians were less likely to be the sole decision makers when purchasing TV or video equipment. This is in keeping with the Aquarius reputation for being egalitarian and preferring to make decisions collectively with others.

Business

Aquarians were more likely to be interested in business-related subjects. Business is not listed as an Aquarian interest by traditional astrologers, but business knowledge overlaps with psychology, which is an Aquarian interest. Moreover, studying business may be a route to self-employment or employment with unconventional companies, both of which are appealing to Aquarians, given the difficulties they have with authority and overly structured environments.

Crafts

Aquarians were more likely to be interested in sewing or knitting. Sewing and knitting are not listed as Aquarian interests in traditional astrology books.

However, most Aquarians are visually oriented and love patterns, which may incline them toward crafts that involve the production of patterned themes.

Alcoholic beverages

Aquarians were more likely to give advice about alcoholic beverages. Wine and spirits are not linked with the sign of Aquarius. However, they are associated with places where people gather to socialize, debate, play games, and make new connections, all of which appeal to the typical Aquarius.

Cooking and baking

Aquarians were more likely to say that they cooked or baked regularly, an unexpected finding given this sign's reputation as non-domestic. However, Aquarians may enjoy preparing food because it provides opportunities to be creative, experimenting with recipes and trying new things.

Technology

Aquarians were more likely to give advice on technology. Technology is associated with the sign of Aquarius, according to traditional astrological wisdom, so this finding is in line with the classic astrological profile for this sign.

Soccer

Aquarians were slightly less likely to play soccer, which is unsurprising, given the association of this sign with winter sports and cycling (Aquarians were more likely than those of other signs to own a mountain bike).

Vintage vehicles

Aquarians were less likely than those of other signs to show an interest in vintage cars or vintage motorcycles, The lack of interest in vintage objects may be attributable to this sign's futuristic orientation (Aquarians tend to like modern things more than old things).

Mountain bikes

Aquarians were more likely to buy mountain bikes. Mountain bikes offer opportunities for freedom, adventure, independence, excitement, and seeing new places while using an environmentally friendly mode of transportation, all of which would appeal to the typical Aquarius.

Astrology

Aquarians were more likely to purchase astrology books, consistent with the assertions of traditional astrologers that Aquarians are open-minded and interested in psychology and occult subjects.

Microwave ovens

Aquarians were less likely to own a microwave oven, in keeping with the Aquarian preference to do things differently and to acquire fewer material things than the average person or collect unusual things rather than ordinary things (Aquarians tend to favor items that support hobbies or sports rather than extra appliances or popular decorative objects, though they may collect unusual décor items).

Higher education

Sachs found that Aquarians were slightly less likely to study law than those of other signs and more likely to study psychology. Although some Aquarians are well-suited to law because they are good arguers, they may dislike working within the restrictive structures of the legal profession. Psychology, on the other hand, is associated with the sign of Aquarius and usually listed as an Aquarian interest in astrology books.

Jobs

Sachs found that Aquarians were more likely to be farmers, architectural draughtsmen/women, physiotherapists, social workers, teachers, and psychologists.

On the other hand, professions in which Aquarians were underrepresented included baker, painter, carpenter, furniture maker, bank clerk, company owner, bookkeeper, computer scientist, interior designer, hairdresser, and chemist.

The only real surprises on these lists are the high rate of farming and the lower likelihood of working as computer scientists. However, farming allows for independent self-employment, which may make agriculture more appealing to independent Aquarians, and computer scientists often have to work in traditional office settings, which would reduce the appeal of this career option.

Chapter 12: Aquarius Stuff

Metal: platinum

Gemstones: aquamarine, garnet (January), amethyst (February)

Parts of the body: achilles tendon, circulatory system, shins, ankles, calves

Number: 4

Places: Sweden, Poland, Zimbabwe, USSR, Ethiopia, Moscow, Hamburg, Stockholm, Buenos Aires, Salzburg

Animals: stag, seahorse, large birds

Trees: pine, rowan, ash

Plants and herbs: comfrey, mandrake, hemp, cannabis, pansies, sorrel, moss

Foods: Spinach, parsnip

Colors: electric blue, purple

Patterns or design motifs: Geometric, psychedelic, outer space

Additional Aquarius associations:

- airplanes
- archeology
- astronomy
- bicycles
- change
- chaos
- comics
- computers
- conspiracy theories
- debates
- democracy
- electronic equipment
- engineering
- gadgets
- games
- humanitarian activities
- inventions
- lava lamps
- neon
- physics
- protests
- psychedelic art and drugs
- radios
- revolutions
- science fiction books and movies
- science in general
- sociology
- spaceships/UFOs

Appendix 1: Famous Aquarians

Famous people with the sun in Aquarius include:

- Abraham Lincoln
- Adam Lambert
- Adlai Stevenson
- Alfred Adler
- Alice Walker
- Alicia Keys
- Andrews Segovia
- Anna Pavlova
- Anton Chekhov
- Arsenio Hall
- Arthur Rubinstein
- Ashton Kutcher
- Axl Rose
- Ayn Rand
- Babe Ruth
- Barbara Tuchman
- Benny Hill
- Betty Friedan
- Bill Maher
- Billie Joe Armstrong
- Bob Marley
- Boris Yeltsin

- Brandon Lee
- Brian Greene
- Burt Reynolds
- Carmen Miranda
- Carol Channing
- Charles Darwin
- Charles Dickens
- Charles Lindbergh
- Chesley Sully Sullenberger
- Chris Farley
- Chris Rock
- Christian Bale
- Christian Dior
- Christie Brinkley
- Christina Ricci
- Christopher Eccleston
- Christopher Marlowe
- Chuck Yeager
- Clark Gable
- Colette
- Corazon Aquino
- Cristiano Ronaldo
- Dan Quayle
- David Lynch
- Denise Richards
- Diane Lane
- Dick Cheney
- Douglas MacArthur
- Dr. Dre
- Duane Chapman
- Eartha Kitt
- Ed Sheeran
- Eddie Izzard
- Eddie Van Halen
- Edith Wharton
- Edwin Buzz Aldrin
- Edwin Newman
- Elijah Wood
- Elizabeth Olsen
- Ellen DeGeneres
- Ernest Bourgnine
- Evangeline Adams
- Farrah Fawcett
- Federico Fellini
- Felix Mendelssohn
- Florence Henderson
- Francis Drake

- Franklin D. Roosevelt
- Franz Schubert
- Frederico Fellini
- Galileo Galilee
- Garth Brooks
- Gary Coleman
- Geena Davis
- Gene Siskel
- George A. Romero
- Germaine Greer
- Gertrude Stein
- Glenn Beck
- Guy Fieri
- Harriet Tubman
- Harry Styles
- Heather Graham
- Helen Gurley Brown
- Hugh Downs
- Ice T
- Jack Benny
- Jack Nicklaus
- Jackie Robinson
- Jackson Pollock
- James Dean
- James Joyce
- James Pike
- Jane Seymour
- Jeb Bush
- Jennifer Anniston
- Jeremy Bentham
- Jerry Sandusky
- Jerry Spinelli
- Jerry Springer
- Jillian Michaels
- Jimmy Hoffa
- Joel Rifkin
- John Belushi
- John Grisham
- John Hancock
- John Hughes
- John Hughes
- John McEnroe
- John Travolta
- John Williams
- Joseph Gordon-Levitt
- Judith Light
- Judy Blume
- Jules Verne

- Justin Timberlake
- Kim Jong-il
- Kim Novak
- Laura Ingalls Wilder
- Lauren Conrad
- Lewis Carroll
- Linda Blair
- Lisa Marie Presley
- Lord Byron
- Manuel Noriega
- Mary Leakey
- Mary Quant
- Matt Dillon
- Matt Groening
- Meg Cabot
- Mia Farrow
- Michael Bay
- Michael Jordan
- Michio Kaku
- Mikhail Baryshnikov
- Mo Willems
- Molly Ringwald
- Nastassja Kinski
- Natalie Cole
- Neil Diamond
- Nicolas Sarkozy
- Norman Mailer
- Norman Rockwell
- Noynoy Aquino
- Oprah Winfrey
- Oral Roberts
- Oscar de la Hoya
- Paris Hilton
- Paul Newman
- Paul Ryan
- Paul Stanley
- Phil Collins
- Philip Glass
- Portia de Rossi
- Princes Charlene of Monaco
- Princess Caroline of Monaco
- Princess Stephanie of Monaco
- Ransom Riggs
- Rebel Wilson
- Richard Dean Anderson
- Robbie Williams

- Robert Burns
- Ronald Reagan
- Ronda Rousey
- Rosa Parks
- Sarah Palin
- Seth Green
- Shakira
- Shannon Hale
- Sidney Sheldon
- Simon Pegg
- Sinclair Lewis
- Sir Francis Bacon
- Sir Francis Galton
- Sonny Bono
- Steve Nash
- Susan B. Anthony
- Susan Sontag
- Tallulah Bankhead
- Taylor Lautner
- Ted Koppel
- Telly Savalas
- Thomas Edison
- Thomas Paine
- Thomas Stonewall Jackson
- Tito Ortiz
- TJ Dillashaw
- Tom Brokaw
- Tom Selleck
- Toni Morrison
- Vanessa Redgrave
- Vanna White
- Victor Ortiz
- Virginia Woolf
- W. C. Fields
- W. Somerset Maugham
- Walter Raleigh
- Wayne Gretzky
- William Burroughs
- Wolfgang Amadeus Mozart
- Wolfman Jack
- Yasser Arafat
- Yoko Ono
- Zane Grey
- Zsa Zsa Gabor

Aquarius Rising (Aquarius Ascendant)

The ascendant is the mask we wear in social situations, or the outer persona we show to others. In the case of Aquarius rising, the external personality will be defined by Aquarius traits, or a blend between Aquarius and the sun sign.

Famous people with Aquarius rising include:

- Alan Arkin
- Billy Ray Cyrus
- Bjorn Borg
- Carl Jung
- Casey Affleck
- Evel Knievel
- Harry Chapin
- Henry Winkler
- Jesse Jackson
- Jim Morrison
- Karl Marx
- Kirk Douglas
- Matt Damon
- Matt Dillon
- Michael J. Fox
- Ralph Nader
- Richie Valens
- Roseanne Barr
- Shaun Cassidy
- Tammy Wynette
- Thomas Jefferson
- Vincent Price
- Wayne Gretzky
- Whoopi Goldberg
- Willem Dafoe
- William Butler Yeats

Appendix 2: Moon Signs, Ascendants (Rising Signs), and Planets

The natal zodiac is like a snapshot of the sky at the moment of birth, and planetary positions in the natal zodiac influence various aspects of personality. The sun, moon, and ascendant (rising sign) are the primary astrological forces, though other planets also play a role. Most people know their sun signs, but few know their ascendants or their other planetary signs.

Astrodienst (www.Astro.com) offers free chart calculation, so you can use this site to find your planetary placements and aspects and your rising sign (for the rising sign, you will need your time of birth as well as the date and place).

The Most Significant Astrological Forces

Most people know their Sun sign, which is the zodiac position of the sun at the time of birth, but few know their rising or moon signs or where their angular planets lie. In fact, the majority of people are surprised to learn that they even have these things.

Of the planetary placements, the sun, moon, and rising signs have the strongest effect on personality. The other planetary placements (positions of the planets at the time of birth) also have effects, though these are not as strong and tend to be concentrated in certain areas rather than shaping the entire personality.

The Sun Sign

The sun sign provides information about basic character and a framework for the rest of the natal zodiac. However, other elements such as the rising sign (also known as the ascendant) and moon sign affect the way the sun sign is expressed.

The Rising Sign (Ascendant)

The rising sign determines the outward expression of personality, or the way in which a person interacts with the external world. It can be described as the public persona or mask. It also indicates how an individual is likely to be perceived by others (how he or she comes across socially).

When the sun and ascendant are in the same or similar signs, a person behaves in a way that is consistent with his or her inner character. When the rising sign is very different from the sun sign, the individual is likely to be pulled in competing directions or to send out signals that don't match inner feelings, which increases the likelihood of being misunderstood by others. While such conflicts can make life difficult, they are also a source of creativity and a spur to achievement.

The Moon

The moon sign is the private persona, only seen in adulthood by those very close to the person. The moon rules over childhood and people are more likely to express their moon sign personalities when they are young. In adulthood, the moon's influence is usually hidden, relegated to the secret emotional life, though an individual may openly express the moon sign persona in times of stress or other emotional extremes.

The moon also represents the mother and other female forces in a person's life. The placement of the moon in a natal chart can indicate the types of relationships and interactions a person is likely to have with women.

Other Planets

Other planets also play a role in shaping the qualities that make up an individual. Each of the planets has a particular sphere of influence, and its effects will be determined by the sign in which the planet falls and the aspects it makes to other planets.

Mercury: all forms of mental activity and communication, including speaking and writing, the intellect, intelligence, reason, perception, memory, understanding, assimilation of information, and critical thinking

Venus: love, affection, pleasure, beauty, sex appeal, art, romantic affairs, adornment, social graces, harmony, and friendship

Mars: physical energy, will power, temper, assertiveness, boldness, competitiveness, impulsiveness, forcefulness, aggression, action, accidents, destructiveness, courage, and sex drive

Jupiter: luck and fortune, optimism, generosity, expansiveness, success, higher education, law, medicine, philosophy, abundance, and spirituality

Saturn: hard work, responsibility, character, strength of will, endurance, hard karma, difficulties, obstacles, hardship, the ability to see a task through to completion, authority, diligence, limitations, self-control, stability, patience, maturity, restriction, and realism

Uranus: progressiveness, change, originality, invention, innovation, technology, science, rebellion, revolution, sudden events and opportunities, awakenings, shocks, flashes of genius, eccentricity, unconventionality, unusual circumstances or events, independence, visionary ideas, and occult interests

Neptune: imagination, intuition, mysticism, dreams, fantasies, compassion, psychic abilities, visions, spirituality, strange events, the subconscious, repressed memories, glamour, mystery, insanity, drama, addiction, ideals, inspiration, transcendence, artistic sensibilities, and creative genius

Pluto: power, transformation, release of dormant forces, change, the subconscious, suppressed energies, death, rebirth, regeneration, sex, jealousy, passion, obsession, intensity, creation and destruction, beginnings and endings that occur simultaneously (one thing ending so that another can begin), secrets, mystery, undercurrents, precognition, personal magnetism, and extremes of personality

House Placements

House placements are a sort of fine tuning, adding some small, specific details about the ways in which various planetary placements will be expressed. The planets represent the spheres of life in which the sign traits are acted out, and the house placements are the stage or setting for these acts.

1st House: self-awareness and self-expression, outer personality, responses to outside stimuli, assertiveness, competitiveness, self-promotion, and courses of action chosen (ruled by mars)

2nd House: material possessions and attitude towards material possessions and money, ability to earn money, extensions of material wealth such as quality of food, decadence, luxury, and physical or external beauty (ruled by Venus)

3rd House: logical and practical reasoning, the intellect, agility, dexterity, curiosity, all forms of communication, all forms of media, intuition about trends and public desires or tendencies, short journeys, and siblings (ruled by Mercury)

4th House: home and hearth, domestic life, domestic chores, family, babies, comfort, the mothering instinct, food, and household items (ruled by the moon)

5th House: creative self-expression, socializing, children, early education, sports, the arts (especially the performing arts), pleasure and places of amusement, parties, social popularity, amd fame (ruled by the sun)

6th House: necessary tasks, details, health consciousness, nutrition, humility, hard work, organization, service, self-control, and sense of duty (ruled by Mercury)

7th House: relationships, friendships, marriage, all forms of partnership (business and social), harmony, balance, conflict avoidance, sense of justice, ideals, the reactions of others to our actions, what attracts us to other people (the sign at the beginning of our seventh house is often the astrological sign we find most attractive), fairness, and aesthetic sense (ruled by Venus)

8th House: legacies, shared resources, taxes, power, death, rebirth, sexuality, the dark side of life, deep psychology, personal magnetism, transformation (self-initiated or imposed by external forces), secrets or secret societies, spying, and prophetic dreaming (ruled by Pluto)

9th House: long distance travel, higher education, religion, medicine, law, animals, knowledge gained through travel and philosophical thinking, high ideals, philanthropy, luck, expansiveness, and ideas about social justice and civilization (ruled by Jupiter)

10th House: career, responsibility, honor and dishonor, perceptions of authority, relationships with authority figures, relationships with business and political power structures, responsibility, hard work, limitations, social standing, public reputation, and business (ruled by Saturn)

11th House: humanitarian endeavors, social ideals, group work, intellectual creative expression, desire to change social and political structures, contrariness, rebelliousness, invention and innovation, progressiveness, change, and personal freedom (ruled by Uranus)

12th House: the subconscious mind, self-sacrifice, intuition, miracles, secret knowledge, martyrdom, spiritual joy and sorrow, imagination, dreams, brilliance, madness, sensation-seeking, self-

destruction, addiction, compassion, kindness, the
ability to transcend boundaries, confusion, deception
(of others and oneself), and altruism (ruled by Neptune)

Angular Planets

Angular planets are planets located along the axis – in other words, planets that fall along the line where the 12th house joins the 1st house, the 3rd house joins the 4th house, the 6th house joins the 7th house, and the 9th house joins the 10th house. Of these, the line that separates the 12th house from the 1st house and the line that separates the 9th house from the 10th house are considered the most important.

Planets that fall where the 12th house joins the 1st house will have a particularly strong effect on overall personality. Planets at this location are called rising planets, so a person with Uranus on the cusp of the 12th and 1st houses will be strong in the areas ruled over by Uranus and show traits of the sign that Uranus rules (Aquarius).

Planets located on the midheaven, which is the cusp of the 9th and 10th houses, also have a very strong effect on certain aspects of personality, particularly career aptitudes and choices. Rising and midheaven planets are some of the most important factors in a person's chart, though IC planets (those located on the cusp of the 3rd and 4th houses) and descending planets (located on the cusp of the 6th and 7th houses) can also have an effect.

The IC provides insights into the self that is seen by those closest to us, such as family, as well as our family structure.

The descendant, or cusp of the 6th and 7th houses, indicates the sorts of people we are attracted to. Theoretically, we should be most attracted to the sign of our descendant (directly opposite our ascendant).

Some astrologers believe that people who have many angular planets are more likely to become famous at some point during their lives.

Aspects

Aspects are the angles the planets formed in relation to one another at the time of a person's birth. The aspects considered most important include the conjunction, sextile, square, trine, inconjunct, and opposition.

Conjunction

A conjunction occurs when two planets are 0 degrees apart – in other words, right next to one another. This powerful aspect is often beneficial, though not always, because if the two planets involved are in negative aspect to many other planets, the conjunction can intensify the problems associated with the difficult aspects.

Planets in conjunction are working together, and their influence will have a major effect on personality. People with planets in conjunction often have one or two extremely well-developed talents or aptitudes, and many people who invent things or are responsible for medical breakthroughs have conjunctions or stelliums (more than two planets in conjunction). Having three or more planets in conjunction can indicate genius in a certain area.

Sextile

A sextile occurs when two planets are 60 degrees apart. Sextiles are beneficial aspects that create opportunities.

Unlike the trine, which simply drops good fortune in a person's lap, the sextile presents opportunities in the areas ruled by the planets involved in the sextile, and it is up to the individual to seize these opportunities and make something of them.

Square

A square occurs when two planets are 90 degrees apart. Squares are stressful or challenging aspects.

Having squares in a natal chart often encourages creativity and ambition, as squares bring obstacles that must be overcome and strife that inspires the individual to develop necessary strengths and use creative problem solving abilities. Squares can promote character development because they ensure that life never becomes too easy.

Trine

Trines occur when two planets are 120 degrees apart. Trines are the most positive and harmonious aspects, bringing good fortune, ease, advantage, and luck in the areas ruled over by the planets involved in the trine.

Inconjunct

An inconjunct occurs when two planets are 150 degrees apart. The effects of the inconjunct are unpredictable, though often problematic.

An inconjunct can indicate stress, health problems, weaknesses, challenges, and obstacles in the personality or the environment that must be overcome. Some astrologers believe that the inconjunct (also known as a quincunx) brings the type of challenges that create wisdom.

Opposition

An opposition occurs when two planets are 180 degrees apart. Oppositions are difficult aspects that can bring discord, stress, chaos, and irritation, but like squares they tend to promote creativity, strength, and character development. It is more productive to view them as challenges rather than problems.

References

Bugler, C. (Ed.). (1992). *The Complete Handbook of Astrology*. Marshall Cavendish Ltd., Montreal.

Castille, D. (2000). *Sunny Day for a Wedding*. Les Cahiers du RAMS.

Fenton, S. (1989). *Rising Signs*. HarperCollins, London.

Heese, A. (2017). Cafe Astrology. CafeAstrology.com.

Quigley, J.M. (1975). *Astrology for Adults*. Warner Books, New York.

Rowe, P. *The Health Zodiac*. Ashgrove Press, Bath.

Sachs, G. (1998). *The Astrology File: Scientific Proof of the Link Between Star Signs and Human Behavior*. Orion Books, London.

Woolfolk, J.M. (2001). *The Only Astrology Book You'll Ever Need*. Madison Books, Lanham, MD.

Image Credits

Image source: http://www.publicdomainfiles.com

- A pair of hearts: Mogwai
- A seahorse at the Georgia Aquarium: Angela Grider
- Abraham Lincoln - 1865: j4p4n
- Alianças (rings): Adassoft
- Aquarius: Lordoftheloch
- Broken heart: Maqndon
- Business people silhouettes: Asrafil
- Hands with hearts: Petr Kratochvil
- Hearts: Vera Kratochvil
- Jigsaw: Yuri1969
- Mother and child silhouette: Warszawianka
- Mountain bike: Zeimusu
- Night sky with moon and stars: George Hodan
- Penguins: Merlin 2525
- Recreation Boise Front Mountain Bikes, Four Rivers Field Office, Lower Snake River District: US Bureau of Land Management
- Stethoscope: Johnny_automatic
- Woman with laptop computer: Petr Kratochvil
  Young girl playing on the beach: CDC / Amanda Mills

CPSIA information can be obtained
at www.ICGtesting.com
Printed in the USA
FFHW011251150319
51105329-56532FF

9 781976 852350